knitbot

essentials

by Hannah Fettig

Nine Classic Designs for the Modern Knitter

with

quince&co.

ISBN 9780985299002
Printed in the United States by Puritan Press

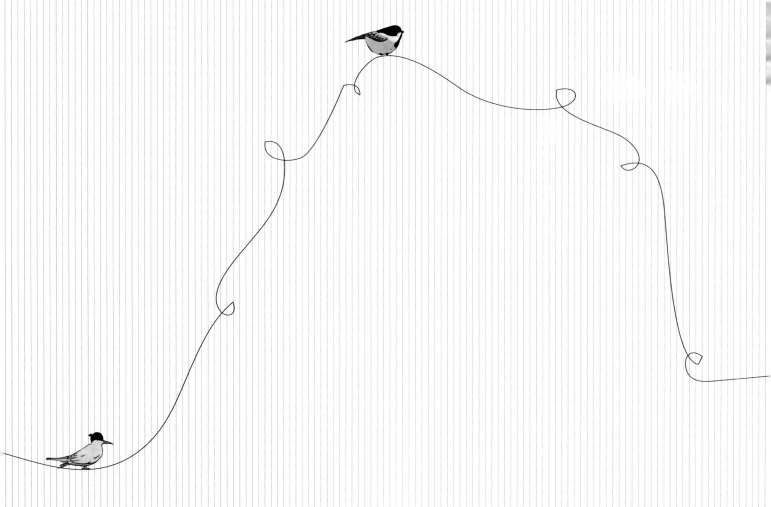

Table of Contents

You meet the nicest people when you have a yarn company. Not long ago, Hannah Fettig stopped by the Quince & Co. warehouse for a visit. She looked around the cluttered front end of our rambling space, spotted a clearing, and asked, "Could I rent a corner here for my office?" To which we replied, "Of course!"

Not long after, a set of Ikea shelves, a long narrow table, and a small lamp with stylized leaves on the shade appeared, as well as a swiveling armchair that has seen better days. Then came boxes of patterns, books, totes tipped with needles and yarn. Finally, a large brown box was delivered. Addressed to Hannah. Inside was a sleek new Herman Miller chair. We gathered to admire it. Hannah had arrived.

We're delighted to share digs with Hannah. What better way to swap ideas? She hadn't been in her new chair for long before ideas for collaboration were flying back and forth. Soon "How about" conversations coalesced into a particular plan, a project—and, finally, this book. A collection of Hannah's lovely, quintessential sweater designs, all knitted in Quince & Co. yarns.

Hannah Fettig has an eye for clean, uncluttered design. She creates simple modern pieces that resonate with women who want to feel pretty and comfortable in what they wear. The clean lines and easy drape of Hannah's signature pieces are the kind of thing you never tire of; you feel splendid in them. Wear them over a nightgown or a little black dress—they work.

Simple, unstructured pieces require yarns that play to drape and movement. Quince & Co. yarns, spun in a small historic mill on turn-of-the-century equipment have an even, balanced twist for a smooth, stable surface, a round structure for body, and plenty of loft for sweaters soft and caressable.

If you don't mind my saying, Hannah's knitwear and Q & Co. yarns—we think we're perfect for each other.

Pam Allen

Chickadee is a little darling—soft, plump, springy, and eager to loop into intricate color patterns or delicate textures. Its three plies, spun from the softest American wool, are twisted firmly enough to be sturdy and definite, yet gently enough to be soft and cushiony.

Finch is a sprite, a fingering-weight with the slightest of halos. It's soft to the touch, yet its neatly twisted plies give it a smooth, tailored finish that's sturdy and hardwearing. It's perfectly balanced for an even stockinette stitch, and you'll love how it shows off texture and lace patterns. Perfect for Fair Isle, too.

Soft and skinny is our wispy *Tern*, a blend of wool and tussah silk. The yarn's muted palette—think vintage painted photographs—results from the different way in which the fibers absorb dye. The wool portion colors thoroughly, but the silk is barely tinted. It's good for socks, scarves, mitts, hats, and any sweater that loves a little drape.

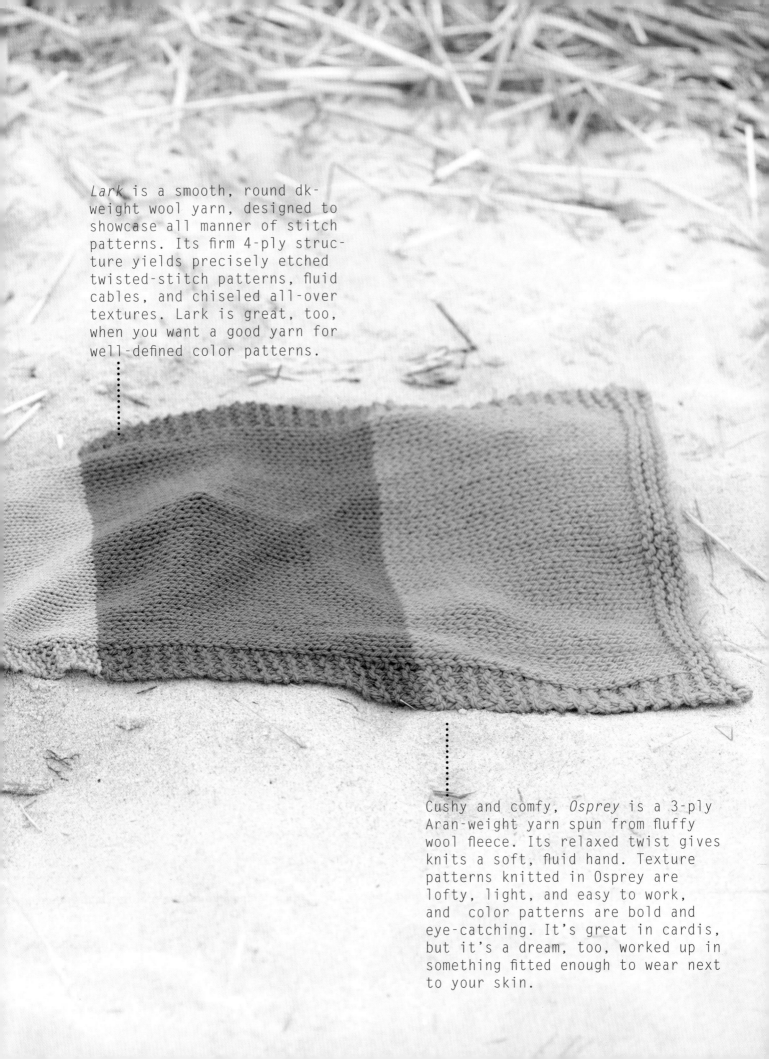

Lark is a smooth, round dk-weight wool yarn, designed to showcase all manner of stitch patterns. Its firm 4-ply structure yields precisely etched twisted-stitch patterns, fluid cables, and chiseled all-over textures. Lark is great, too, when you want a good yarn for well-defined color patterns.

Cushy and comfy, *Osprey* is a 3-ply Aran-weight yarn spun from fluffy wool fleece. Its relaxed twist gives knits a soft, fluid hand. Texture patterns knitted in Osprey are lofty, light, and easy to work, and color patterns are bold and eye-catching. It's great in cardis, but it's a dream, too, worked up in something fitted enough to wear next to your skin.

A lesson in drape

The history.
Since I first began designing I have been interested in knit fabrics with drape. One of the first yarns I ever played with was Rowan Kidsilk Haze. A friend I had taught to knit called me almost in tears after I recommended this yarn to her. "It's like knitting with cobwebs!" she lamented. Oh, but the things you could create with this cobweb.

My first popular design was Whisper Cardigan, which appeared in the Spring 2009 issue of Interweave Knits. When designing this piece I considered all the layering pieces I owned and discovered most of them were drapey cottons and jersey. I was inspired to replicate the feel of this fabric in my knitting. Lace weight yarn on a size 7 needle took me there.

After the success of Whisper I designed Featherweight Cardigan, a simple top down raglan cardigan featuring the same fabric as Whisper. It turned out I wasn't alone in my love of this piece. Many, many Featherweight Cardigans have been successfully knit and worn by knitters around the world!

For Effortless Cardigan, I bumped up the yarn weight and needle size, knitting with DK weight yarn on a size 9 needle. Knitters could once again achieve fantastic drape through use of a loose gauge.

Creating your fabric.
To knit each pattern successfully, you need to get gauge. However, you can choose how whispery or drapey you want your piece to be by playing with your yarn choice. For example, Featherweight, Wispy and Breezy Cardigans were originally designed with lace weight yarn on a size 6 or 7 needle. For this collection these designs are presented in fingering weight yarn. Drape is still achieved but the fabric is a little more substantial, less whispery. Effortless Cardigan can be knit with either DK or worsted weight yarn, depending on how much drape you'd like.

It all leads you to one task: swatching.

Knitting your swatch.
Most of the pieces in this collection feature drape. To achieve this you will be using a needle size larger than recommended on the ball band. It is most important that you check your gauge, especially if you are substituting yarns for those suggested in this book.

Start with the needle size recommended in the pattern. Knit a generous stockinette stitch swatch. If you can be patient enough to also block your swatch, this will give you a truer sense of the gauge. Don't be surprised if you have to go up or down a needle size, maybe even two. If you are usually a tight or a loose knitter, this can be exaggerated by the loose gauge.

Most of the patterns do not have you go down a needle size for ribbing as the ribbing is intended not to pull in at all. However if you feel like your ribbing looks too loose when knitting feel free to go down a needle size.

What size should I knit?
For any of the cardigans, if you are in between sizes I recommend choosing the smaller size over the larger size. Too much extra fabric may feel fussy or cumbersome. If you tend to like your garments oversized, I think you'll find that the drape that is built into the design will feel comfortable to you if you stick to your appropriate size.

The Sweaters

Wispy

This is a variation of Whisper Cardigan which appeared in the Spring 2009 issue of Interweave Knits. When designing Whisper I thought about the layering pieces that were part of my wardrobe, all of which were cotton or jersey with drape. I tried to replicate the feeling of these pieces in this design. This sample is knit in fingering weight yarn. Lace weight yarn can also be used.

Sizes
Child's 4/6 (8/10, 12/14, Women's S, M, L, XL, XXL)

Finished measurements
Chest/bust circumference: 25 (28, 31, 34, 38, 42, 46, 50)"
Shown in size Women's Small, 34" with 2" positive ease. See Pattern Notes regarding measurements.

Yarn
Quince and Company *Finch* (100% American wool, 221yd [202m]/50g); 3 (4, 5, 5, 6, 7, 8, 8) skeins in Glacier 106 or 650 (875, 1050, 1050, 1300, 1500, 1750, 1750) yds of lace or fingering weight yarn.

Needles
US6 / 4 mm 24" circular needle or straight needles
US4 / 3.5 mm 24" circular needle
US2 / 2.75 mm circular or straight needles
Adjust needle size to obtain correct gauge.

Notions
Stitch markers (m), tapestry needle

Gauge
24 sts and 36 rows = 4"/ 10 cm in stockinette stitch using largest needle

Pattern Notes
There are 3 steps to knitting Wispy. First, the shrug part of the cardigan is worked from side to side. Second, the collar and waist are picked up around the opening of the shrug. Third, the body of the cardigan is knit down from the waist.

The measurements listed are the actual measurements of the cardigan, from armhole to armhole, NOT the measurement across your back from armpit to armpit. To figure out which size to knit, put your arms at their sides. (You might need some help with this one!) Start measuring from the side of your left arm, then across the back of your arm, across your back, across the back of your right arm, finishing the measurement at the side of your right arm.

Because the cardigan is knit from side to side, you can try it on as you go and make adjustments.

Begin right sleeve
With largest needles cast on 60 (66, 72, 78, 88, 96, 106, 114) sts.

Work in k1, p1 rib for 1.5".

Work in St st until sleeve measures 6 (7, 8, 9, 9, 9.5, 9.5, 10)" or desired length, ending with a WS row.

Bind off 6 (7, 8, 9, 11, 13, 15, 17) sts at the beg of the next 2 rows. 48 (52, 56, 60, 66, 70, 76, 80) sts.

Shrug body
Continue working back and forth in St st for 8.75 (9.75, 11, 12, 13, 14, 15, 16)", or desired length, ending with a WS row.

Note: You can try the shrug on as you go for a custom fit! You are aiming for your middle back at this point.

Gathering at middle back
RS: With smallest needles, k2tog to end of row. 24 (26, 28, 30, 33, 35, 38, 40) sts.
WS: Purl to end.
RS: K1, M1 to last st, kfb. 48 (52, 56, 60, 66, 70, 76, 80) sts.

With largest needles, work in St st for 8.75 (9.75, 11, 12, 13, 14, 15, 16)", or length to match the right half of the back, ending with a WS row.

Begin left sleeve
Using the backward loop method, cast on 6 (7, 8, 9, 11, 13, 15, 17) sts at the end of the next 2 rows. 60 (66, 72, 78, 88, 96, 106, 114) sts.

Work in St st for 4.5 (5.5, 6.5, 7.5, 7.5, 8, 8, 8.5)", or length to match the right sleeve before rib.

Work in k1, p1 rib for 1.5". Bind off loosely in rib.

Seam sleeves.

Collar and waist
With middle sized needles and starting with the left sleeve, pick up and knit 10 (12, 14, 16, 20, 24, 28, 32) sts along left underarm, 2 sts for every 3 rows along base of the shrug, 10 (12, 14, 16, 20, 24, 28, 32) sts along the right underarm, pm, then 2 sts for every 3 rows along the top of the shrug (see techniques page 47). Pm and join to work in the round.

Note: The exact number of stitches doesn't matter, as long as it is an even number.

Work in k1, p1 rib for 2 (2.5, 2.5, 3, 3, 3, 3, 3)".

Final round: Work in rib to marker, bind off across the top of the shrug to end of round.

Body of cardigan
With largest 24" needles, work short row shaping as follows:

Slip 1, k3, w&t, p to end.
Slip 1, k7, w&t, p to end.
Slip 1, k11, w&t, p to end.
Slip 1, k15, w&t, p to end.

Note: When you are knitting across a wrapped stitch, pick up the wrap and knit it together with the stitch.

Slip 1, k1, M1L, k across all remaining sts to last 2 sts, M1R, k2.
Slip 1, p3, w&t, k to end.
Slip 1, p7, w&t, k to end.
Slip 1, p11, w&t, k to end.
Slip 1, p15, w&t, k to end.

Note: When you are purling across a wrapped stitch, pick up the wrap and purl it together with the stitch.

Slip 1, p to end of row.

Continue in this manner:

RS: Slip 1, k1, M1L, k to last 2 sts, M1R, k2.
WS: Slip 1, purl to end of row.
Repeat these 2 rows for 5 (6, 7, 8, 8.5, 9, 9.5, 10)" or desired length.

Work in k1, p1 rib for 1.5". Bind off loosely in rib.

Finishing
Weave in all ends. Block lightly to measurements.

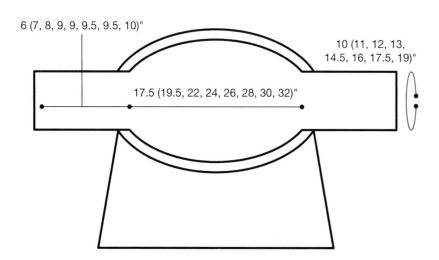

Featherweight

After the success of Whisper, I set out to design another layering cardigan with the same lightweight fabric. Featherweight is a simple top down raglan with a wide collar. The cardigan is so basic you can use it as a template: play with the sleeve and body length, knit in solid or stripes, pick a textured or lace stitch pattern for the collar. Make it your own! This sample is knit in fingering weight yarn. Lace weight yarn can also be used.

Finished measurements
Bust: 32 (35.25, 38.75, 42, 45.25)[48.75, 52, 55.25, 58.75, 62]"
Length: 15.5 (16.75, 18, 19, 20.25)[21.5, 22.5, 23.75, 25, 26]"
Sample shown is 35.25 with 3.25" positive ease.

Yarn
Quince and Company *Tern* (75% American wool, 25% silk; 221yd [202m]/50g); 4 (4, 5, 6, 6)[7, 8, 9, 10, 10) skeins in Boothbay 145 or 800 (875, 1100, 1200, 1300)[1500, 1700, 1900, 2100, 2200) yds of lace or fingering weight yarn.

Needles
US6 / 4 mm needles:
• 32" circular
• double-pointed needles (dpns)
Adjust needle size to obtain correct gauge.

Notions
Stitch markers (m), stitch holders or waste yarn to hold sleeve sts, tapestry needle

Gauge
24 sts and 36 rows = 4" / 10 cm in stockinette stitch

Begin at top
Cast on 52 (54, 56, 58, 60)[62, 64, 66, 68, 70] sts.

Setup row (WS): P2 (front), pm, p2 (sleeve), pm, p44 (46, 48, 50, 52)[54, 56, 58, 60, 62] (back), pm, p2 (sleeve), pm, p2 (front).

Row 1 (RS): (K to 1 st before m, M1R, k1, sm, k1, M1L) 4 times, k to end. 8 sts increased.
Row 2: Purl. (see techniques page 47, for M1L and M1R)

Repeat these two rows 24 (27, 30, 33, 36)[39, 42, 45, 48, 51] times more. 252 (278, 304, 330, 356)[382, 408, 434, 460, 486] sts: 27 (30, 33, 36, 39)[42, 45, 48, 51, 54] front sts, 52 (58, 64, 70, 76)[82, 88, 94, 100, 106] sleeve sts, 94 (102, 110, 118, 126)[134, 142, 150, 158, 166] back sts.

Divide sleeves from body
Next row (RS): (Knit to marker, remove marker, place sleeve sts on a holder, remove marker, cast on 2 (4, 6, 8, 10)[12, 14, 16, 18, 20] underarm sts, knit to end. 152 (170, 188, 206, 224)[242, 260, 278, 296, 314] body sts.

Work even in St st until piece measures 8 (8.5, 9, 9.5, 10)[10.5, 11, 11.5, 12, 12.5]" from underarm to bottom edge, or 2" less than desired length.

Continue in k1, p1 rib for 2" or desired length. Bind off loosely in rib.

Sleeves
Slip held sleeve sts onto dpns. With RS facing, k52 (58, 64, 70, 76)[82, 88, 94, 100, 106] sleeve sts, then pick up and knit 2 (4, 6, 8, 10)[12, 14, 16, 18, 20] sts along cast on sts at underarm, placing marker in middle of picked up sts. Join for working in the round. 54 (62, 70, 78, 86)[94, 102, 110, 118, 126] sts.

Work even in St st for 11 (11, 11, 9, 9)[7, 7, 5, 5, 5] rounds.

Decrease round: K1, ssk, k to last 3 sts, k2tog, k1.
2 sts decreased.

Repeat this decrease round every 12 (12, 12, 10, 10)[8, 8, 6, 6, 6] rounds 5 (5, 5, 7, 7)[9, 9, 11, 11, 13] times more. 42 (50, 58, 62, 70)[74, 82, 86, 94, 98] sts.

Work even until sleeve measures 9 (9, 9, 9, 10)[10, 10, 11, 11, 11]" or 2" less than desired length.
Work in k1, p1 rib for 2" more.

Bind off loosely in rib.

Collar

Starting at right front bottom edge, pick up 2 sts for every 3 rows of the right front edge. (see techniques, page 47) Continue across the top of the right sleeve, across the back, then across the top of the left sleeve, picking up 1 st for every st. Finish by picking up 2 sts over every 3 rows along left front edge.

Work collar in St st until collar measures 3.5" or desired length.

Bind off loosely.

Note: Don't want your collar to roll? Try it in k1, p1 rib or a lace stitch pattern!

Finishing

Weave in all ends. Block to measurements.

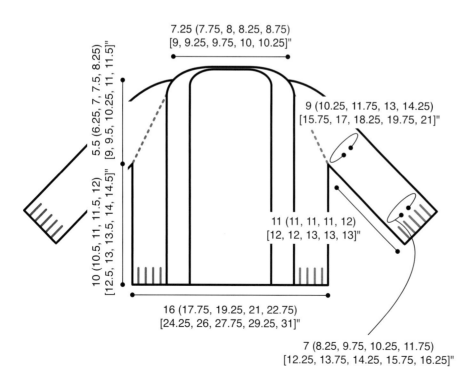

7.25 (7.75, 8, 8.25, 8.75) [9, 9.25, 9.75, 10, 10.25]"

5.5 (6.25, 7, 7.5, 8.25) [9, 9.5, 10.25, 11, 11.5]"

9 (10.25, 11.75, 13, 14.25) [15.75, 17, 18.25, 19.75, 21]"

10 (10.5, 11, 11.5, 12) [12.5, 13, 13.5, 14, 14.5]"

11 (11, 11, 11, 12) [12, 12, 13, 13, 13]"

16 (17.75, 19.25, 21, 22.75) [24.25, 26, 27.75, 29.25, 31]"

7 (8.25, 9.75, 10.25, 11.75) [12.25, 13.75, 14.25, 15.75, 16.25]"

Effortless

Effortless is all about drape. It's a seamless cardigan knit from the top down, featuring wide front panels that naturally fall open. This piece offers grace and comfort—the perfect cardigan! This sample is knit in worsted weight yarn, but gauge can also be achieved with dk weight yarn. Even with the bands of ribbing that are picked up and knit for the collar, this is a fast knit!

Finished measurements

Chest circumference: 30.5 (34.5, 38.5, 42, 46.5, 50.5)"
Length: 21.5 (22.5, 23.5, 24.75, 25.75, 26.75)"
Sample shown is size 34.5" with 2.5" positive ease.

Yarn

Quince and Company *Lark* (100% American wool, 134yds [123m]/50g); 8 (9, 10, 11, 12, 14) skeins in Storm 104 or 1000 (1125, 1300, 1450, 1600, 1775) yards of dk or worsted weight yarn.

Needles

US9 / 5.5 mm needles:
• double-pointed needles (dpns)
• 24–40" circular depending on chest circumference

Adjust needle size to obtain correct gauge.

Notions

Stitch markers (m), stitch holder, tapestry needle

Gauge

19 sts and 26 rows = 4" / 10 cm in stockinette stitch

Begin at top

With circular needle, cast on 48 (60, 64, 74, 78, 88) sts.

Setup row (WS): P3 (front), pm, p7 (9, 9, 11, 11, 13) (sleeve), pm, p28 (36, 40, 46, 50, 56) (back), pm, p7 (9, 9, 11, 11, 13) (sleeve), pm, p3 (front).

Raglan increases

RS: K1, M1L, (knit to 1 st before m, M1R, k1, sm, k1, M1L) four times, knit to 1 st from end of row, M1R, k1.
10 sts increased.
WS: Purl to end.

Repeat the last two rows 17 (18, 20, 21, 23, 25) times more. 228 (250, 274, 294, 318, 348) sts: 39 (41, 45, 47, 51, 55) front sts, 43 (47, 51, 55, 59, 65) sleeve sts, 64 (74, 82, 90, 98, 108) back sts.

RS: K1, M1L, (knit to 1 st before m, M1R, k1, sm, k1, M1L) 4 times, knit to 1 st from end of row, M1R, k1, then using the backward loop method cast on 27 (30, 31, 34, 35, 36) sts.
WS: P to end, then using the backward loop method cast on 27 (30, 31, 34, 35, 36) sts.
292 (320, 346, 372, 398, 430) sts: 68 (73, 78, 83, 88, 93) front sts, 45 (49, 53, 57, 61, 67) sleeve sts, 66 (76, 84, 92, 100, 110) back sts.

Divide sleeves from body

RS: K68 (73, 78, 83, 88, 93), remove marker, place 45 (49, 53, 57, 61, 67) sleeve sts on a stitch holder, cast on 3 (3, 4, 4, 5, 5) sts, pm, cast on 3 (3, 4, 4, 5, 5) sts, knit across 66 (76, 84, 92, 100, 110) back sts, remove marker, place 45 (49, 53, 57, 61, 67) sleeve sts on a stitch holder, cast on 3 (3, 4, 4, 5, 5) sts, pm, cast on 3 (3, 4, 4, 5, 5) sts, k68 (73, 78, 83, 88, 93). 214 (234, 256, 274, 296, 316) sts.

Continue in St st until sweater measures 1.5 (2, 2, 2.5, 2.5, 3)" from underarm.

Decrease row (RS): (Knit to 3 sts before m, k2tog, k1, sm, k1, ssk) twice, knit to end. 4 sts decreased.

Repeat this *decrease row* every 12th row 2 times more. 202 (222, 244, 262, 284, 304) sts.

Work in St st for 1".

Increase row (RS): (Knit to 1 st before m, M1R, k1, sm, k1, M1L) twice, knit to end. 4 sts increased.

Repeat this *increase row* every 12th row 2 times more. 214 (234, 256, 272, 296, 316) sts.

Continue in St st until body measures 11.5 (12, 12.5, 13, 13.5, 14)" from underarm, or 3" less than desired length.

Work in k2, p2 rib for 3". Bind off loosely in rib.

Sleeves

Place 45 (49, 53, 57, 61, 67) held sleeve sts on dpns, ready to be worked. Pick up and knit last 3 (3, 4, 4, 5, 5) of the 6 (6, 8, 8, 10, 10) cast on sts from underarm, k45 (49, 53, 57, 61, 67), pick up and knit first 3 (3, 4, 4, 5, 5) underarm sts, pm, join for working in the round. 51 (55, 61, 65, 71, 77) sts.

Work in St st for 7 rounds.

Decrease round: K1, ssk, knit to last 3 sts, k2tog, k1. 2 sts decreased.

Repeat this *decrease round* every 10 (9, 8, 7, 6, 5) rounds 5 (6, 7, 8, 9, 10) times more. 39 (41, 45, 47, 51, 55) sts.

Work even until sleeve measures 13", or 3" less than desired length.

Next round: Dec 3 (1, 1, 3, 3, 3) sts evenly around. 36 (40, 44, 44, 48, 52) sts.

Work in k2, p2 rib for 3". Bind off loosely in rib.

Finishing

Note: For bands and collar, the exact number of stitches doesn't matter, as long as it is divisible by two.

Bands

With longer circular needles and starting at the lower edge of the right front panel, pick up and knit 2 sts for every 3 rows to the top edge (see techniques, page 47). Work in k2, p2 rib for 3". Bind off loosely in rib.

Starting at the upper edge of the left front panel, pick up and knit 2 sts for very 3 rows to the bottom edge. Work in k2, p2 rib for 3". Bind off loosely in rib.

Collar

Starting at the right corner, pick up and knit 2 sts for every 3 rows across the top of the band, then pick up 1 st for every st across the right front panel, across the top of the sleeve, across the back, across the left sleeve, across the left front panel, then 2 sts for every 3 rows across the left panel band. (see techniques, page 47)

Work in k2, p2 rib for 3". Bind off loosely in rib.

Weave in all ends. Block to measurements.

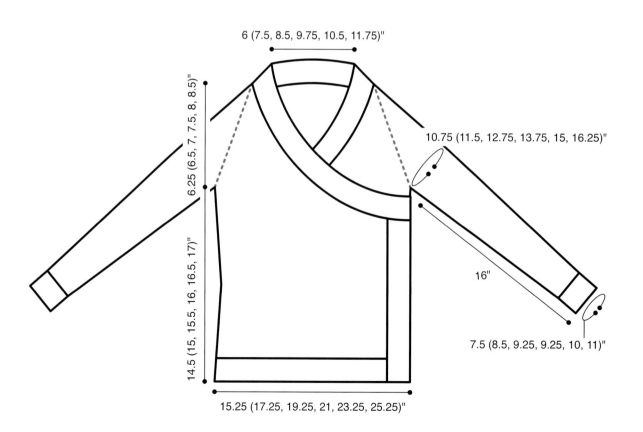

6 (7.5, 8.5, 9.75, 10.5, 11.75)"

6.25 (6.5, 7, 7.5, 8, 8.5)"

10.75 (11.5, 12.75, 13.75, 15, 16.25)"

14.5 (15, 15.5, 16, 16.5, 17)"

16"

7.5 (8.5, 9.25, 9.25, 10, 11)"

15.25 (17.25, 19.25, 21, 23.25, 25.25)"

Breezy

What would happen if Featherweight and Effortless became one design? Breezy! Beautiful fields of Stockinette stitch knit in lace or fingering weight yarn drape at the front in such a pleasing manner. This seamless top down cardigan requires knitting a lot of stockinette stitch and a lot of ribbing for the collar. If you really enjoy the rhythm of mindless knitting this is the project for you! This sample is knit in fingering weight yarn. Lace weight yarn can also be used.

Finished measurements
Chest: 34.75 (38, 41.25, 44.75, 48)[51.25, 54.75, 58, 61.25]"
Length: 22 (23.25, 24.25, 25.5, 26.75)[27.75, 29, 30.25, 31.25]"
Shown in size 34.75" with 2.75" of positive ease.

Yarn
Quince and Company *Tern* (75% American wool, 25% silk; 221yd [202m]/50g); 6 (7, 8, 9, 10)[11, 12, 13, 14) skeins in Barnacle 139 or 1300 (1500, 1700, 1900, 2100)[2300, 2500, 2700, 2900) yds of lace or fingering weight yarn.

Needles
US6 / 4 mm needles:
• 2 16" circulars or set of double-pointed needles (dpns)
• 32–40" circular for body, collar and bands
Adjust needle size to obtain correct gauge.

Notions
Stitch markers (m), stitch holders, tapestry needle

Gauge
24 sts and 36 rows = 4" / 10 cm in stockinette stitch

Begin at top

With longer circular needles, cast on 78 (80, 82, 84, 86)[88, 90, 92, 94] sts.

Setup row

WS: P4 (front), pm, p12 (sleeve), pm, p46 (48, 50, 52, 54)[56, 58, 60, 62] (back), pm, p12 (sleeve), pm, p4 (front).

RS: K1, M1L, (knit to 1 st before m, M1R, sm, k1, M1L) 4 times, knit to 1 st from end of row, M1R, k1. 10 sts increased (see techniques, page 47 for M1L and M1R).
WS: Purl to end.

Repeat the last two rows 25 (28, 31, 34, 37)[40, 43, 46, 49] times more. 338 (370, 402, 434, 466)[498, 530, 562, 594] sts: 56 (62, 68, 74, 80)[86, 92, 98, 104] front sts, 64 (70, 76, 82, 88)[94, 100, 106, 112] sleeve sts, 98 (106, 114, 122, 130)[138, 146, 154, 162] back sts.

RS: Knit to end of row, then using the backward loop method cast on 38 (40, 42, 44, 46)[48, 50, 52, 54] sts.
WS: Purl to end, then using the backward loop method cast on 38 (40, 42, 44, 46)[48, 50, 52, 54] sts. 414 (450, 486, 522, 558)[594, 630, 666, 702] sts: 94 (102, 110, 118, 126)[134, 142, 150, 158] front sts, 64 (70, 76, 82, 88)[94, 100, 106, 112] sleeve sts, 98 (106, 114, 122, 130)[138, 146, 154, 162] back sts.

Divide sleeves from body

RS: (Knit to marker, place sleeve sts on a piece of stitch holder, removing markers, cast on 3 (4, 5, 6, 7)[8, 9, 10, 11] sts, pm, cast on 3 (4, 5, 6, 7)[8, 9, 10, 11] sts) twice, knit to end. 298 (326, 354, 382, 410)[438, 466, 494, 522] sts.

Continue in St st until sweater measures 2″ from underarm.

Decrease row (RS): (Knit to 3 sts before m, k2tog, k1, sm, k1, ssk) twice, knit to end. 4 sts decreased.

Repeat this *decrease row* every 2″ twice more. 286 (314, 342, 370, 398)[426, 454, 482, 510] sts.

Work in St st for 1″.

Increase row (RS): (Knit to 1 st before m, M1R, k1, sm, k1, M1L) 2 times, knit to end. 4 sts increased.

Repeat this *increase row* every 2″ once more. 294 (322, 350, 378, 406)[434, 462, 490, 518] sts.

Continue in St st until body measures 12 (12.5, 13, 13.5, 14)[14.5, 15, 15.5, 16]″ from underarm, or 3″ less than desired length.

Work in k2, p2 rib for 3″. Bind off loosely in rib.

Sleeves

Place 64 (70, 76, 82, 88)[94, 100, 106, 112] held sleeve sts on dpns. Knit across, then pick up 6 (8, 10, 12, 14)[16, 18, 20, 22] cast on sts at underarm, placing marker at center of picked up sts.
70 (78, 86, 94, 102)[110, 118, 126, 134] sts.

Join for working in the round.

Work in St st for 11 rounds.

Decrease round: K1, ssk, knit to last 3 sts, k2tog, k1.
2 sts decreased.

Repeat this *decrease round* every 14 (11, 9, 8, 7)[6, 5, 5, 4] rounds 5 (7, 9, 11, 13)[15, 17, 19, 21] times more. 58 (62, 66, 70, 74)[78, 82, 86, 90] sts.

Work even until sleeve measures 13″, or 3″ less than desired length.

Work in k2, p2 rib for 3″. Bind off loosely in rib.

Finishing
Bands
With longer circular needle and starting at the lower edge of the right front panel, pick up and knit 2 sts for every 3 rows to the top edge. (see techniques, page 47)

Note: For bands and collar, the exact number of stitches doesn't matter, as long as it is divisible by four.

Work in k2, p2 rib for 3". Bind off loosely in rib.

Starting at the upper edge of the left front panel, pick up and knit 2 sts for very 3 rows to the bottom edge. Work in k2, p2 rib for 3". Bind off loosely in rib.

Collar
With longer circular needle and starting at the right corner, pick up and knit 2 sts for every 3 rows across the top of the band, then pick up and knit1 st for every st across the right front panel, across the top of the sleeve, across the back, across the left sleeve, across the left front panel, then pick up and knit 2 sts for every 3 rows across the left panel band.

Work in k2, p2 rib for 3". Bind off loosely in rib.

Seam sleeves. Weave in all ends. Block to measurements.

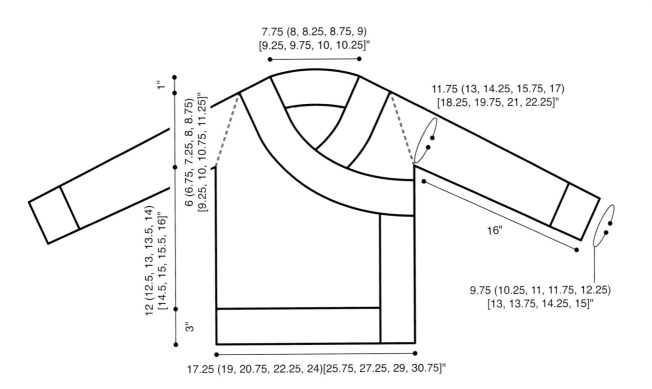

7.75 (8, 8.25, 8.75, 9) [9.25, 9.75, 10, 10.25]"

11.75 (13, 14.25, 15.75, 17) [18.25, 19.75, 21, 22.25]"

1"

6 (6.75, 7.25, 8, 8.75) [9.25, 10, 10.75, 11.25]"

12 (12.5, 13, 13.5, 14) [14.5, 15, 15.5, 16]"

16"

3"

9.75 (10.25, 11, 11.75, 12.25) [13, 13.75, 14.25, 15]"

17.25 (19, 20.75, 22.25, 24)[25.75, 27.25, 29, 30.75]"

Lightweight

With some successful cardigans under my belt, I wanted to design a pullover. Lightweight is a seamless raglan, knit from the top down beginning with the cowl neck. This sample is knit with dk weight yarn at the recommended gauge. For a truly lightweight pullover, try getting gauge with fingering or lace weight yarn!

Finished measurements
Bust: 35.25 (38.75, 42, 45.25, 48.75, 52)"
Length: 20.75 (21.75, 23, 24.5, 25.75, 27.5)"
Shown in size 35.25" with 3.25" positive ease.

Yarn
Quince and Company *Chickadee* (100% American wool, 181yd s[166m]/50g); 8 (9, 10, 11, 12, 13) skeins in Bird's Egg or 1400 (1550, 1750, 1900, 2150, 2350) yds of fingering or dk weight yarn.

Needles
US6 / 4 mm needles:
• 16" circular needle
• set of double-pointed needles (dpns)
• 32–40" circular depending on
  bust circumference
Adjust needle size to obtain correct gauge.

Notions
Stitch markers (m), stitch holders, tapestry needle

Gauge
24 sts and 36 rows = 4" / 10 cm in stockinette stitch

Begin at top of collar
With 16" circ, cast on 116 (120, 124, 128, 132, 136) sts. Pm and join for working in the round, being careful not to twist sts. Work in St st in the round for 9".

Setup round: K12, pm, k46 (48, 50, 52, 54, 56), pm, k12, pm, k46 (48, 50, 52, 54, 56), pm.

Begin raglan increases
Note: Switch to longer circ when necessary.
Round 1: (K1, M1L, knit to 1 st before marker, M1R, k1, sm) 4 times. 8 sts increased.
Round 2: Knit to end of round.

Repeat these two rounds 26 (30, 34, 38, 42, 46) times more. 332 (368, 404, 440, 476, 512) sts: 66 (72, 82, 90, 98, 106) sleeve sts and 100 (110, 120, 130, 140, 150) front and back sts.

Divide sleeves from body
K66 (74, 82, 90, 98, 106), place these sleeve stitches on a holder, remove marker, using the backward loop method cast on 3, k100 (110, 120, 130, 140, 150), cast on 3, k66 (74, 82, 90, 98, 106), place these sleeve stitches on a holder, pm, cast on 3, knit to end of round, cast on 3, pm. This is the new beginning of the round. 212 (232, 252, 272, 292, 312) sts.

Work in St st until piece measures 2 (2, 2.5, 3, 3.5, 4)" from underarm.

Decrease round: (K2, ssk, knit to 4 sts before marker, k2tog, k2, sm) 2 times, knit to end of round. 4 sts decreased.

Repeat this *decrease round* every 2" twice more. 200 (220, 240, 260, 280, 300) sts.

Work in St st for 1".

Increase round: (K2, M1L, knit to 2 sts before m, M1R, k2, sm) 2 times, knit to end of round. 4 sts increased.

Repeat this *increase round* every 2" twice more. 212 (232, 252, 272, 292, 312) sts.

Continue in St st until the body measures approx 11 (11, 11.5, 12, 12.5, 13)" or 4" less than desired length.

Work in k2, p2 rib for 4".
Bind off loosely in rib.

Sleeves
Slip 66 (74, 82, 90, 98, 106) held sleeve sts onto dpns. With right side facing, pick up and knit first 3 of the 6 cast on sts at underarm, pm, pick up and knit 3 remaining sts from cast on at underarm, join for working in the round, knit around sleeve sts to m. 72 (80, 88, 96, 104, 112) sts.

Work in St st for 11 rounds.

Decrease round: K1, ssk, knit to last 3 sts, k2tog, k1. 2 sts decreased.

Repeat this *decrease round* every 12 (12, 10, 8, 8, 8) rounds 6 (6, 8, 10, 12, 14) times more. 58 (66, 70, 74, 78, 82) sts.

Work even until sleeve measures 13 (13, 13.5, 14, 14.5, 15)" or 4" less than desired length.

Next round: K1, ssk, knit to last 3 sts, k2tog, k1. 2 stitches decreased.

Work in k2, p2 rib for 4". Bind off loosely in rib.

Finishing
Weave in all ends. Block to measurements.

19.25 (20, 20.75, 21.25, 22, 22.75)"

9"

5.75 (6.75, 7.5, 8.5, 9.25, 10.25)"

12 (13.25, 14.75, 16, 17.25, 18.75)"

15 (15, 15.5, 16, 16.5, 17)"

17 (17, 17.5, 18, 18.5, 19)"

9.75 (11, 11.75, 12.25, 13, 13.75)"

35.25 (38.75, 42, 45.25, 48.75, 52)"

Trail Jacket

After designing so many lightweight pieces, I was inspired by Quince and Company's Osprey to try an Aran weight knit. The Trail Jacket is easy to wear, and can add a tailored look to your outfit. Worked from the top down, there is a slight flare to the body and sleeves. Garter stitch graces the cuffs, hem, collar and button bands. This is a chance to showcase some fantastic buttons, such as the wooden ones on this sample.

Finished measurements
Chest: 33.25 (37.75, 41.25, 45.75, 50.25, 53.75, 58.25)"
Length: 19.5 (21, 21.25, 22.75, 23.25, 25.25, 27.5)"
Shown in size 33.25"shown with 2" positive ease.

Yarn
Quince & Company *Osprey* (100% Wool; 170yds [155m]/100g); 4 (5, 5, 6, 7, 8, 9) skeins in Pea Coat 110 or 680 (850, 850, 1020, 1190, 1360, 1530) yds of Aran weight yarn.

Needles
US10.5 / 6.5 mm:
• 32" circular needle
• set of double-pointed needles (dpns)
Adjust needle size to obtain correct gauge.

Notions
Stitch markers (m), 5 (5, 5, 5, 6, 6, 6) 1.5" diameter buttons, stitch holder, tapestry needle

Gauge
14 sts and 20 rows = 4" / 10 cm in stockinette stitch

Pattern Notes
Raglan increases and button holes are worked at the same time, so read pattern carefully before beginning.

Begin at top
With circ needle, cast on 34 (38, 46, 48, 58, 58, 64) sts.

Setup row (WS): P3 (front), pm, p4 (4, 6, 6, 8, 8, 10) (sleeve), pm, p20 (24, 28, 30, 36, 36, 38) (back), pm, p4 (4, 6, 6, 8, 8, 10) (sleeve), pm, p3 (front).

RS: K1, M1L, (knit to 1 st before m, M1R, k1, sm, k1, M1L) four times, knit to last st of row, M1R, k1. 10 sts increased.
WS: Purl to end of row. (see techniques, page 47 for M1L and M1R)

Repeat these two rows 4 (4, 4, 6, 6, 8, 8) times more. 84 (88, 96, 118, 128, 148, 154) sts: 13 (13, 13, 17, 17, 21, 21) front sts, 14 (14, 16, 20, 22, 26, 28) sleeve sts, 30 (34, 38, 44, 50, 54, 56) back sts.

Cast on sts for fronts
RS: (Knit to 1 st before m, M1R, k1, sm, k1, M1L) four times, knit to end of row, then using the backward loop method cast on 8 (10, 12, 13, 16, 16, 17) sts.
WS: Purl to end of row, then using the backward loop method cast on 8 (10, 12, 13, 16, 16, 17) sts. 108 (116, 128, 152, 168, 188, 196) sts: 22 (24, 26, 31, 34, 38, 39) front sts, 16 (16, 18, 22, 24, 28, 30) sleeve sts, 32 (36, 40, 46, 52, 56, 58) back sts.

RS: (Knit to 1 st before m, M1R, k1, sm, k1, M1L) four times, knit to end of row. 8 sts increased.
WS: K8, purl to last 8 sts of row, k8.

Repeat these two rows 9 (11, 12, 12, 13, 13, 16) times more. 188 (212, 232, 256, 280, 300, 332) sts: 32 (36, 39, 44, 48, 52, 56) front sts, 36 (40, 44, 48, 52, 56, 64) sleeve sts, 52 (60, 66, 72, 80, 84, 92) back sts.

AT THE SAME TIME work buttonhole over the first 8 sts (the garter stitch band) on the RS row 4 rows from the top, then every 16 (18, 18, 20, 16, 18, 20) rows 4 (4, 4, 4, 5, 5, 5) times more as follows:
RS: K3, work buttonhole (see techniques, page 47), k1.

Divide sleeves from body
RS: (Knit to m, remove m, place sleeve sts on a holder, using the backwards loop method cast on 2 sts, pm, cast on 2 more sts) 2 times, knit to end. 124 (140, 152, 168, 184, 196, 212) sts.
WS: K8, purl to last 8 sts, k8.

Continue as established, working body in St st and bands in garter stitch, remembering to work buttonholes, until piece measures 2" from underarm.

Increase row: (Knit to 1 st before m, M1R, k1, sm, k1, M1L; 2 times, knit to end. 4 sts increased.

Repeat this *increase row* every 2" three times more. 140 (156, 168, 184, 200, 212, 228) sts.

Continue in St st until piece measures about 10.5 (11.25, 10.75, 11.5, 11.25, 12.5, 13.25)", from underarm, ending 5 rows after working a buttonhole.

Work in garter stitch for 2". Bind off all sts.

Sleeves

Place 36 (40, 44, 48, 52, 56, 64) sts from holder on dpns. Pick up and knit first 4 sts of the 8 cast on sts from the underarm, pm, pick up and knit last 4 sts, join for working in the round. 40 (44, 48, 52, 56, 60, 68) sts.

Work in St st for 4".

Decrease round: K1, ssk, knit to last 3 sts, k2tog, k1. 38 (42, 46, 50, 54, 58, 66) sts.

Continue until sleeve measures 9" from underarm.

Work in garter st for 2". Bind off all sts.

Finishing
Collar

With RS facing and starting at right front, pickup and knit 8 (10, 12, 13, 16, 16, 17) sts along top of band, then pickup and knit 5 (5, 5, 7, 7, 9, 9) sts, along right neck edge to cast on sts, pick up and knit 1 st for every st, cast on 5 (5, 5, 7, 7, 9, 9) sts along left front neck, and 8 (10, 12, 13, 16, 16, 17) sts along top of left band. 60 (68, 80, 88, 104, 108, 116) sts. (see techniques, page 47)

Work in garter st for 2". Bind off all sts.

Weave in all ends. Block to measurements. Sew buttons to band opposite buttonholes.

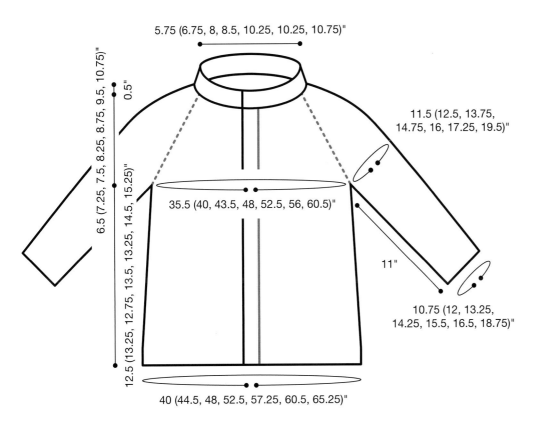

5.75 (6.75, 8, 8.5, 10.25, 10.25, 10.75)"

6.5 (7.25, 7.5, 8.25, 8.75, 9.5, 10.75)"

0.5"

11.5 (12.5, 13.75, 14.75, 16, 17.25, 19.5)"

35.5 (40, 43.5, 48, 52.5, 56, 60.5)"

12.5 (13.25, 12.75, 13.5, 13.25, 14.5, 15.25)"

11"

10.75 (12, 13.25, 14.25, 15.5, 16.5, 18.75)"

40 (44.5, 48, 52.5, 57.25, 60.5, 65.25)"

The Accessories

Day Beret

This beret was the first design in my Knitbot Snack Size Pattern Series. This pattern series was a small collection of quick to knit staple accessories. I certainly didn't invent the stockinette stitch beret. But sometimes as knitters we want basic, especially when we have a gorgeous yarn or colorway to showcase! This simple beret is sized for children and adults, with instructions to enlarge the adult size if you want it to be a little roomier.

Finished measurements

Child's version
Brim circumference: 15.25"
Widest point circumference: 23"
Height: 6"

Adult version
Brim circumference: 17.5"
Widest point circumference: 26"
Height: 8.5"

Yarn
Quince and Company *Chickadee* (100% American wool, 181yds [166m]/50g); 1 skein in Pomegranate 112 or 115 (180) yds of dk weight yarn.

Needles
US 3 / 3.25 mm 16" circular needle
US 5 / 3.75 mm
• 16" circular needle
• set of double-pointed needles (dpns) for the final decrease rounds
Adjust needle size to obtain correct gauge.

Notions
Tapestry needle, 12 (15) stitch markers (m)

Gauge
23 sts and 32 rows = 4" / 10cm in stockinette stitch

Beret
With smaller circular needles cast on 88 (100) sts.
Join for working in the round, being careful not to twist sts, pm to mark the beginning of the round.

Setup round: (K1, p1) repeat to end.
Continue in k1, p1 rib for 6 (10) rounds, or desired length.

Switch to larger circular needles.
Knit 1 round.

Increase rnd: (K1, kfb) repeat to end. 132 sts (150) sts.

Continue in St st, until hat measures 3.5 (5.5)" from cast on edge, or desired length.
Note: if you want to make your hat bigger, this is where you do it! Work 4 – 6 extra rounds in St st. Consider the above listed finished measurements carefully before doing this.

Setup round: [K11 (15) pm) repeat to end.
Decrease round: (K to 2 sts before m, ssk, sm) repeat to end.
12 (10) sts decreased.
Repeat this *decrease round* every other round until 12 (10) sts remain.
(Note: Switch to dpns when sts can no longer stretch around circular needles.)
Final round: (K2tog) repeat to end.

Finishing
Cut yarn and thread onto tapestry needle. Pull the tail through remaining sts and weave it into the wrong side of the hat. Weave in all ends. Block to measurements.

Tricolor Cowl

The second project from my Knitbot Snack Size Pattern Series is this simple cowl. It features 3 tiers of lace or fingering weight yarn. Light and airy, it's comfortable enough to wear all day. A great project to use up leftover balls of yarn. (You know you have plenty of those rolling around your house!)

Finished measurements
Circumference: 18"
Length: 9"

Yarn
Color 1: Quince and Company *Tern* (75% American wool, 25% silk; 221yd [202m]/50g) ; 1 skein in Buoy 144 or 60 yds of lace or fingering weight yarn.
Color 2: Quince and Company *Tern* (75% American wool, 25% silk; 221yd [202m]/50g); 1 skein in Back Bay 148 or 60 yards of lace or fingering weight yarn.
Color 3: Quince and Company *Tern* (75% American wool, 25% silk; 221yd [202m]/50g); 1 skein in Oyster 142 or 60 yards of lace or fingering weight yarn.

Needles
US 3 / 3.25 mm 16" circular needle
US 6 / 4 mm 16" circular needle
Adjust needle size to obtain correct gauge.

Notions
Stitch marker (m), tapestry needle

Gauge
24 sts and 32 rows = 4" / 10cm in stockinette stitch

Cowl
With smaller circular needles and Color 1, cast on 108 sts. Join for working in the round, being careful not to twist sts, pm to mark beginning of round.

Ribbing setup round: (K2, p2) repeat to end.
Continue in k2, p2 rib for 8 rounds.

Switch to larger circular needles.
Knit 16 rounds, or until cowl measures 3" from cast on edge.

Switch to Color 2.
Knit for 24 rounds, or until cowl measures 6" from cast on edge.

Switch to Color 3.
Knit for 16 rounds.

Switch to smaller circular needles.

Ribbing setup round: (K2, p2) repeat to end.
Continue in k2, p2 rib for 8 rounds, or until cowl measures 9" from cast on edge.

Bind off loosely in rib.

Finishing
Weave in all ends.
Block to measurements.

70 Yard Mitts

The third project from my Knitbot Snack Size Pattern Series is this pair of minimalist mitts. No joke—they only require 70 yards of worsted weight yarn. A truly snack size project, you can knit them in one sitting. Add some pops of color to your attire—make a few pair!

Finished measurements
Hand circumference: 7"

Needles
US 3 / 3.25 mm set of double-pointed needles (dpns)
US 6 / 4 mm set of double-pointed needles (dpns)

Notions
2 Stitch markers (m), 2 stitch holders, tapestry needle

Yarn
Quince and Company *Lark* (100% American wool, 134yds [123m]/50g); 1 skein in Honey 123 or approx 70 yds of worsted weight yarn.

Gauge
20 sts and 28 rows = 4" / 10cm in stockinette stitch

Begin mitt
Starting with smaller dpns, cast on 32 sts onto one dpn. Divide sts evenly over 3 dpns.
Join for working in the round, being careful not to twist sts, pm to mark the beginning of the round.

Setup rnd: (K1, p1) repeat to end.
Continue in k1, p1 rib for 9 rounds more.

Switch to larger dpns.
Knit 14 sts, pm, k2, pm, k to end.

Thumb gusset *increase round*: K to m, sm, M1L, k to m, M1R, sm, k to end. 2 sts increased.
Repeat this *increase round* every 3 rounds until there are 12 sts between markers.
Work 2 rounds even.

Divide thumb from mitt
K to m, remove m's, place 12 thumb sts on a holder, using the backwards loop cast on method cast on 2 sts over gap, k to end. 32 sts.
Work even for 4 rounds.

Switch to smaller dpns.
Ribbing setup round: (K1, p1) repeat to end.
Continue in k1, p1 rib for 6 rounds more.
Bind off loosely in rib.

Thumb
Divide 12 thumb sts evenly over 3 smaller dpns. Pickup and knit 2 sts along edge of gap.
Join for working in the round, pm to mark the beginning of the round. 14 sts.

Ribbing setup round: (K1, p1) repeat to end.
Continue in k1, p1 rib for 6 rounds more.
Bind off loosely in rib.

Finishing
Weave in all ends. Block.

Abbreviations

garter stitch: Knit all rows when working flat. Alternate knit 1 round, purl 1 round when working in the round.

k: knit

k2tog: knit two stitches together

kfb: knit into the front and back of the same stitch to create 2 stitches

m: marker

M1L: make one left increase

M1R: make one right increase

p: purl

p2tog: purl two stitches together

pm: place marker

RS: right side

sm: slip marker

ssk: Slip the first stitch as if to knit, slip the second stitch as if to knit, then slide the left needle into the front part of both stitches and knit them together.

St st: Stockinette stitch. Knit on the right side, purl on the wrong side. When working in the round, knit all rounds.

st(s): stitch(es)

WS: wrong side

w&t: wrap and turn. RS facing: with yarn in front, slip the next stitch knitwise from the left to the right needle. Move yarn to back. Slip stitch back from the right to the left needle. Turn work. One stitch has been wrapped. WS facing: with yarn in back, slip the next stitch purlwise from the left to the right needle. Move yarn to front. Slip stitch back from the right to the left needle. One stitch has been wrapped.

Two-row buttonhole

1. With RS facing, move yarn to front. Slip 1 st from the left to the right needle.

2. Move yarn to back. Slip 1 st purlwise from the left to the right needle. Pass first slipped stitch over the second slipped stitch. Repeat 2 times more, a total of 3 sts bound off. Slip the last stitch you bound off back to the left needle and turn your work.

3. With WS facing, cast 4 sts onto your left needle using a knitted cast on. Turn your work.

4. With RS facing, slip 1 st purlwise from the left to the right needle. Pass the last cast on st over the slipped st.

Pick up stitches along a horizontal edge

Pick up and knit one st for each bound off st along your edge. For a nice clean edge, be sure to pick up the complete bound off st, not half of it.

Pick up stitches along a vertical edge

Pick up and knit two sts for every 3 rows. For a nice clean edge, be sure to pick up between the two stitches closest to the edge, not in the middle of the one st closest to the edge.

Make one left increase

Make one st by lifting the bar between sts from front to back with the left needle. Knit through the back of it with the right needle.

Make one right increase

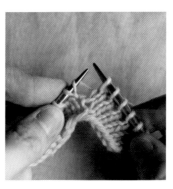

Make one st by lifting the bar between sts from back to front with the left needle. Knit through the front of the st with the right needle.

47

Bios

Hannah Fettig
designs knitwear in Portland, Maine. She is the author of Closely Knit and co-author of *Coastal Knits*, the smash self-published hit released in fall 2011. Her designs have also appeared in *Interweave Knits*, *Knitscene* and *Knitty* magazines. You can view her full line of Knitbot patterns and obtain wholesale information at www.knitbot.com.

Quince and Company
is the result of many "Wouldn't it be great if…" conversations among three yarnophiles. We're two knitwear designers and the owner of a spinning mill, and we each confess to a strong bias toward natural fibers. In 2010, we combined efforts to create a line of thoughtfully conceived quality yarns spun from American wool or sourced from overseas suppliers who grow plants, raise animals, or manufacture a yarn in as earth- and labor-friendly a way as possible. Today we ship yarn all over the world—from Tanzania to Korea to Argentina. Find out more at www.quinceandco.com.

Credits

styling Pam Allen & Hannah Fettig

shoot assistant & technical editor Cecily Glowik MacDonald

photographer & graphic designer Carrie Bostick Hoge

location Black Point Inn

book printing Puritan Press

schematics Mary Joy Gumayagay

technical editor Tana Pageler

illustrations Neesha Hudson

sample knitters Jenna Beegle, Nicole Dupuis, Vanessa Espinosa, Deirdre Kennedy, Peter Kennedy, Andrea Sanchez